Hot Flash Gal

First published in 2004 by Conari Press,
an imprint of Red Wheel/Weiser, LLC
York Beach, ME
With offices at:
368 Congress Street
Boston, MA 02210
www.redwheelweiser.com

ISBN 1-57324-970-X

Typeset in Schmelvetica by Kathleen Wilson Fivel

Printed in China
EVB

11 10 09 08 07 06 05
  8 7 6 5 4 3 2

Hot Flash Gal

Photos by
Kelly Povo

Words by
Phyllis Root
& Kelly Povo

CONARI PRESS

Have you been
dressing in layers lately?

Are you spending
more time on ice?

Do you need
more than a little help
from your friends?

Is your girlish figure
harder to find?

Have your
heating bills
plummeted?

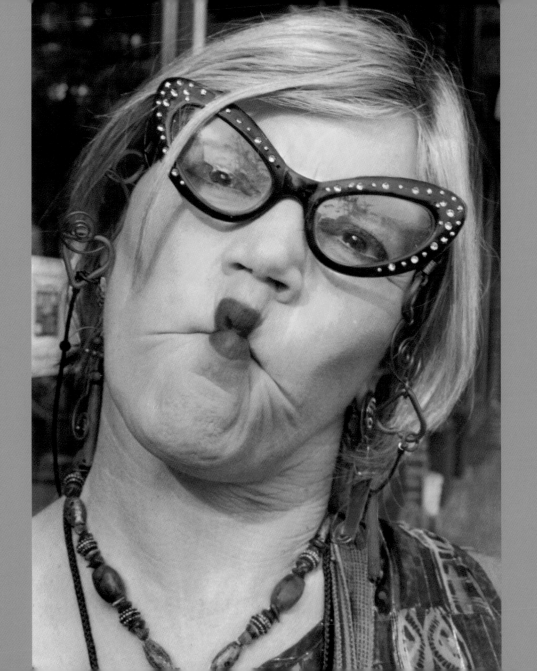

Congratulations!

You're a genuine
HOT FLASH GAL!

Fur coats?
Hot flash gals
don't need
no fur coats.

The hell with sensible shoes!

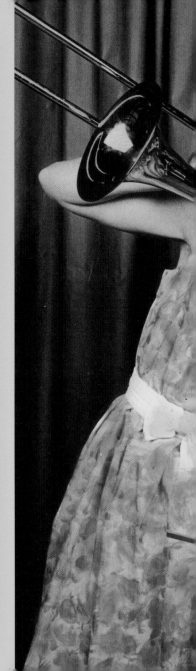

Who needs rhythm?
Hot flash gals
got menopause.

They make friends
wherever they go.

Facial hair?
What facial hair?

Hot flash gals
have a real blast.

Hot flash gals
demand the best.

They insist
on a balanced diet,

fruits and veggies every day,

and plenty
of calcium.

They make sure
to exercise,

and never forget
to moisturize!

Hot flash gals
make the best friends.

Tell them
anything.
They'll never
remember it.

They aren't afraid
to speak their minds.

They know
exactly what
you need.

They stick up for you,
no matter what.

Hot flash gals
won't ever let you down.

So pucker up,
hot flash gal.

Spread
your
wings!

Rev
your
engines!

Strut

your

stuff!

You're getting hot
and loving it.

Nothing
can stop
you now!

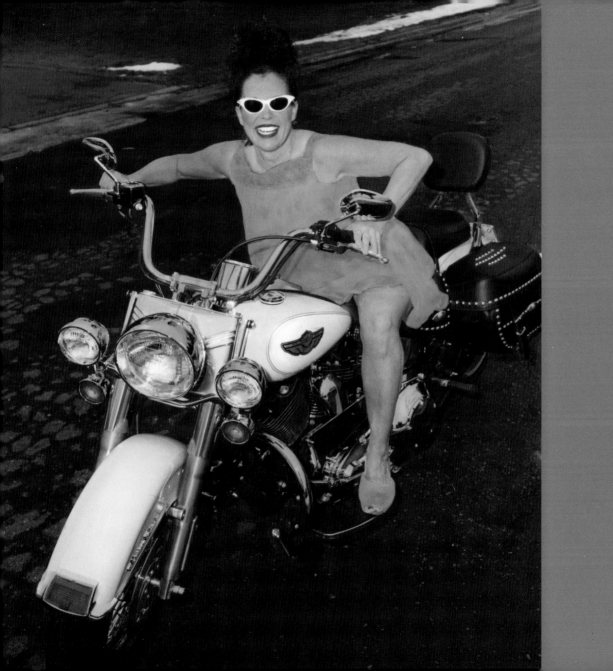

Kelly Povo has been taking
pictures for 20 years, while Phyllis
Root has been writing children's
books. They have been friends
for many years and spend most
of their time together laughing,
even though they don't always
remember what was so funny.